As We Forgive Those

A play

Andrew Smith

Samuel French — London
www.samuelfrench-london.co.uk

ISBN 978 0 573 13206 3

Please see page iv for further copyright information

AS WE FORGIVE THOSE

First presented at Brooklands College Drama Studio, Weybridge, on 5th February 2008 with the following cast:

Alex	Lauren Morley
Sophie	Anna Bonnett
Jen	Emma Nicholson

Directed by Iain Patterson

CHARACTERS

Sophie, early 20s
Alex, her sister, late teens
Jen, Sophie's flatmate, early 20s

The action of the play takes place in the living-room of Sophie's and Jen's flat.

Time — the present

AUTHOR'S NOTE

As We Forgive Those contains infrequent use of strong language, reflecting the way I believe these characters would speak. However, if you would like to remove the swearing (eg. for a school production), I am happy for directors to replace these words with suitable alternatives.

Andrew Smith

The use of a forward slash (/) in certain lines indicates that the next person to speak begins talking at this point, creating overlapping dialogue.

For Amelia and James

AS WE FORGIVE THOSE

A simple, uncluttered living-room with a sofa and coffee table. Upstage is a coat stand and a small side table with a phone on it. Early evening. The room is dark, although some light spills in from a street lamp outside

A girl, Alex, sits apprehensively. She is in her late teens, rather dirty and scruffy in appearance, wearing a hooded jumper. She has a bag

After a long pause, we hear a front door open and shut. Sophie enters and switches on the light. She is in her early twenties and smartly dressed, having just come home from work. She hangs up her coat and puts down her keys. She has a scar on her cheek

Alex Sophie?

Sophie turns to see Alex

Surprise.
Sophie How did you get in?
Alex Pleased to see me?
Sophie *How did* you *get in?*
Alex You left the kitchen window open.
Sophie It's the middle of winter, I did not leave the window open.
Alex Well that's how I got in.

Sophie storms off to the kitchen. She returns immediately

OK, look, I helped it open with a hammer.
Sophie Get out.
Alex I'll pay for it.

Sophie GET OUT.
Alex Can't we sit down?
Sophie Don't you dare. You get out now or I'm / calling the police.
Alex We can talk. Why d'ya wanna do that?
Sophie I don't want you in my house.
Alex Give me five minutes and then I'll go.
Sophie How did you know I live here?
Alex What?
Sophie How did you find me?
Alex I just ... knew.
Sophie I've only been here a few weeks.
Alex So?
Sophie Most of my friends don't know I'm here, so how did you find me?
Alex I don't know, I just found you.
Sophie Don't lie. How did you find me?
Alex I don't know.
Sophie ANSWER ME.
Alex I ... I just saw you.
Sophie Where?
Alex In town. I ... in town, somewhere, I saw you, OK?
Sophie When?
Alex Yesterday.
Sophie And then what? You followed me?
Alex No, I —
Sophie *Then how did you know where I live?*
Alex Yeah, OK, I followed you. I saw you come here, I thought it must be your flat. OK?

Pause

Sophie I *am* calling the police. (*She reaches for the phone*)
Alex Why?! I ain't done nothing.
Sophie You've followed me and broken into my house, that's enough.
Alex For fuck's sake.
Sophie Don't say that.

Alex What?
Sophie (*into the phone*) Police.
Alex Soph, don't do this, don't call the police, please.
Sophie Stay there.
Alex Soph, please. I'll leave if you don't want me here. I'll get my bag now. Don't call the police.
Sophie (*into the phone*) I'd like to report a break-in.
Alex Don't be stupid. Sophie, I need your help. I need your help, OK? I'm in trouble, and I need you to help me, you're the only one I can turn to. Please? (*Beat*) I'm your sister.

Pause. Sophie hangs up the phone

Sophie Why should I help you, after what you did?
Alex I know I ain't got no right to be here, and you probably never wanted to see me again but I didn't know what else to do.
Sophie I'm surprised you can even look at me.

Silence

So what do you want?
Alex Somewhere to stay.
Sophie No way.
Alex Just for a week ... a few days, and then I'll go, I promise.
Sophie No way.
Alex Please, I can pay you.
Sophie I don't want your money —
Alex A hundred, two hundred.
Sophie — I just don't want you here.
Alex Money ain't a problem.
Sophie Then get a hotel.
Alex Is this what Christian charity is?

Beat

Sophie Don't start.

Alex I thought you were supposed to lend a hand to those in need, give shelter to the poor.
Sophie How can you stand there and say that?
Alex Ain't that what Jesus said?
Sophie How would you know anything about that?
Alex Because you used to quote it to me every day of my life.
Sophie If you want me to help you, you're going about it the wrong way.
Alex I just thought I could rely on you for a bit of charity, but obviously not.

Pause

Sophie Where've you been staying?
Alex I was ... living with some mates. I left.
Sophie Why?
Alex Does it matter?
Sophie It does to me.
Alex What is this?
Sophie Do you want me to help you or not?

Beat

Alex I ... fell out with them. I didn't want to stay there any more, so I left. OK?

Beat

Sophie Are you doing drugs?
Alex No.
Sophie You're not taking drugs?
Alex I just told you.
Sophie How do I know you're not on the run?
Alex Who from?
Sophie I don't know. The police, or the people you lived with.
Alex I'm not.

Sophie How do I know?

Alex I'm not like that.

Sophie Like what?

Alex Like, you know, in trouble. I don't do things like that no more. I've changed. You've just gotta believe me. I'm not in trouble with the police, I swear.

Sophie Then why were you so desperate for me not to call them earlier?

Alex Why d'ya think? Because I don't want to get in trouble with them again, and I know what I did was wrong, breaking in here — they'd've nicked me.

Sophie Look, why don't you go and stay in a hostel for a few days? If money's not a problem you'll be fine for a while. This is too much.

Alex I've got no money. I lied. (*She points to her bag*) This is ... everything.

Pause

Sophie Why did you come to me?

Alex I didn't come to you, I found you.

Sophie How lucky for you.

Alex What's that supposed to mean?

Sophie Come here.

Alex *What's that supposed to mean?*

Sophie Come here. I want you to look me in the eye.

Alex I don't need a lecture.

Pause. Eventually, Alex gives in and goes to Sophie

Sophie You can stay here. You can stay here for a week. But I want you to look me in the eye and promise me that you're not involved in anything — crime, drugs, anything like that. Promise me I won't be hiding a criminal in my house.

Pause

Alex I ain't done nothing wrong. I promise.

Sophie If I find out you've lied, I don't care that you're family, I'm calling the police. Is that clear?

Beat

You can sleep on the sofa. And you're / leaving next Monday.
Alex (*indicating the sofa*) On that?!
Sophie What?
Alex Look at the size of it.
Sophie It's that or the floor.
Alex How the hell —
Sophie Take it or leave it.

Beat

Alex Will your flatmate mind?
Sophie Not if it's only for a — . How do you know I've got a flatmate?
Alex Well I ... I just presumed, you know, that you'd have one. It's a big flat.
Sophie Right ... I'm sure she won't mind.
Alex Is she ... around tonight?
Sophie She'll be home soon.

An awkward silence

Do you need a toothbrush, or clothes or anything?
Alex Yeah, that'd be good.
Sophie I'll sort something out for you.
Alex Cheers.

Sophie exits

Nice place.
Sophie (*off*) Nothing special. It's home.
Alex Is it yours?
Sophie (*off*) I bought it, yeah.

Alex You must be doing well for yourself.
Sophie (*off*) Not especially, but I survive.
Alex What do you do?
Sophie (*off*) I'm a teacher.
Alex What, with little kids?
Sophie (*off*) Big kids.
Alex What do you teach?
Sophie (*off*) R.E.

Alex laughs

Why's that funny?
Alex It's not, it's just ...
Sophie (*off*) What? It's just what?
Alex What I expected.

Alex finds a picture of Sophie and her mum on the table. She stares at it

Sophie (*off*) I enjoy what I do.
Alex Good for you.

Sophie returns with pyjamas and a toothbrush for Alex

Sophie One of us had to do something with our life.
Alex You don't look like a teacher.
Sophie What's that supposed to mean?
Alex I dunno ... I just remember most of my teachers being about fifty.
Sophie I'm surprised you were at school long enough to notice.
Alex You just look too young.
Sophie I'm old enough.
Alex You ain't changed.

Sophie stares at Alex. Alex looks away

Sorry.

Pause

How is Mum?
Sophie Do you care?
Alex I'm just asking, you don't have to spit everything back at me.
Sophie Mum's coping. Is that all right?
Alex Does she hate me?
Sophie I don't know. Why don't you ask her?

Pause

No, she doesn't hate you. She couldn't hate you — you're her daughter. She's been desperate to find you. She prays for you every day, hoping you're safe and that you'll just walk through the front door one night. You're still her little girl.
Alex And you?
Sophie What about me?
Alex Have you prayed for me?

Beat

Sophie I've prayed *about* you.
Alex Maybe God's listened.
Sophie Call Mum will you? Let her know you're OK.
Alex I don't know her number.
Sophie I'll give you the number. Please call her.
Alex I'll do it later.
Sophie Promise?
Alex What is it with you and promises? I'll do it later.

Beat

When did you say your flatmate would be back?
Sophie Soon. Does it matter?
Alex No, I just wanted to know. (*She starts to light a cigarette*)
Sophie She normally walks home from work but she's getting a cab tonight, so she'll be in a bit earlier. You're not smoking in here.

Alex puts the cigarette away

Alex Why's she getting a cab?
Sophie I'm sure she'll tell you. (*Beat*) Are you hungry? I can make you something.
Alex No, I'm fine.
Sophie You can help yourself to anything in the fridge ... the top half. Don't touch anything else.
Alex Cheers.

Pause

What's her name?
Sophie Who?
Alex Your flatmate.
Sophie Jen.
Alex Jen what?

A door opens and closes off stage

Sophie You can ask her yourself.
Alex Can I use your loo?
Sophie Don't you want to say hello?
Alex I just need to ... sort myself out.

Alex exits to the bathroom

Jen enters. She is also in her early twenties, and despite being smartly dressed perhaps lacks the sophistication of Sophie

Jen The bloody taxi driver got lost.
Sophie Did he?
Jen She. It was a she. Sort of ruined the point of me ordering a bloody taxi in the first place. I was stood outside on the corner by my office looking like a hooker, people beeping me and stuff. Do I look like a cheap whore, in a suit?

Sophie Are you OK?
Jen It's freezing out there.
Sophie Did the police get back to you about last night?
Jen No, they're worse than useless. They eventually get through to me at work and say, "We've been trying to contact you all morning but your mobile just keeps going to voicemail", and I say, "That's 'cos my mobile's been stolen you muppet". We *pay* for these people.
Sophie No luck then?
Jen They said, "Oh this kind of thing happens all the time, so it's unlikely we'll get anywhere", as if they've given up. I gave them a description, but they'll probably just use it to draw one of those stupid photofits that makes every suspect look like a Picasso painting. Sod it.
Sophie Jen.
Jen What? Can I not say "sod"? I thought sod was all right. Don't they use "sod" in the Bible?
Sophie I ... maybe, I don't know, I just don't like it.
Jen I'll cross it off the list then.

Pause. Jen thinks

They do use "sod" in the Bible. I can't believe you never swear. Not even when you stub your toe, or see your phone bill?
Sophie Never.
Jen You're weird. Some guy at work pinched my arse today and I slapped him so hard he couldn't say anything but fu — the "f" word — for the rest of the day. I'm gonna get some food.

Jen heads towards the kitchen. A toilet flushes off stage

Who's that? I didn't know you had company. Do you want me to get out your way?
Sophie No, no, it's fine.
Jen Who is it?

Beat

Sophie My sister.
Jen I didn't know you had a sister.
Sophie Well, I do.
Jen You've never mentioned a sister.
Sophie Well, I have one, OK? She's here.
Jen Never mentioned her. Are you all right?
Sophie Yeah. I just ... wasn't expecting her.
Jen A surprise visit!
Sophie Sort of.
Jen Look, I'll leave you to it if you like. I'll go round Tina's house.
Sophie I told Alex she could stay here until Monday, on the couch.
Jen What?!
Sophie She doesn't have to.
Jen How's she supposed to sleep on that?! Look at the size of it!
Sophie It's that or the floor. Look, she'll keep out of your way. I've told her she's got to be out by next Monday.
Jen It's your flat.
Sophie Yeah, but you pay rent. I want to know you're OK with it.
Jen It's a week. As long as she doesn't eat my food!
Sophie I've already told her — top part of the fridge only.
Jen Then we'll get along fine.

Jen exits to the kitchen. Shortly after, Alex returns

Alex Where is she then?
Sophie In the kitchen. I'll introduce you in a sec.
Alex I borrowed your deodorant. Have you told her I'm here?
Sophie Yes.
Alex And?
Sophie And what?
Alex And does she mind?
Sophie It's my flat, I can have who I want here.
Alex And do you want me here?
Sophie I've told you, it's not a problem.
Alex That's hardly a "yes" is it?
Sophie What's up with you?

Alex I get nervous round new people.
Sophie Jen's lovely.

Alex paces uneasily

Jen enters, stuffing her face with cheese

Jen I borrowed some cheese, I hope you don't mind.
Sophie Jen, this is my sister, Alex. Alex, this is Jen.
Jen Nice to meet you.

Alex avoids eye contact

Alex All right?
Jen I didn't know Soph had a sister. She never mentions you.
Alex Right.
Jen I hear you're staying for a few days.
Alex Yeah, if that's all right.
Jen No worries. Just to warn you though, I look like a swamp beast in the morning, so don't be too alarmed if you see a hideous monster crawl through here to the bathroom.

No reaction

So what do you do?
Alex Nothing. I'm looking for a job.
Jen Do you live far away?
Alex No.
Jen How long have you been here?
Alex Where?
Jen In town.
Alex I just got here.
Jen Today?
Alex Yeah.
Jen Cool.

Pause

Sophie I thought you said you got here yesterday.
Alex Eh?
Sophie You told me you got here yesterday.
Alex No I didn't.
Sophie You said you *saw* me yesterday. / And then you ——
Alex I *saw* you, yeah ——
Sophie Yeah, and then / you ——
Alex Yeah, but I didn't stay here. I was here but I didn't stay here. I stayed somewhere else.
Sophie Where did you stay?
Alex With a friend.

An awkward pause. Jen keeps looking at Alex

You got a problem?
Jen What?
Alex You keep staring at me.

Sophie senses something is wrong

Sophie (*to Alex*) Why don't you go and get something to eat?
Alex I'm not hungry.
Sophie Something to drink then.
Alex I don't want anything.
Sophie Well make me a cup of tea, I'd quite like one.
Alex (*under her breath*) Jesus.

Alex exits towards the kitchen

Sophie I'm really sorry about her — she said she gets nervous round new people. I'm sure she didn't mean to sound rude. She doesn't have to stay here if you don't want her to.

Pause

What's up?

Jen Nothing.

Sophie Come on, I'm not stupid.

Jen It's nothing.

Sophie You *were* staring at her.

Jen I'm probably seeing things, it's my bloody imagination playing up again.

Sophie What do you mean?

Jen No, it's stupid. She's your sister. I'm probably getting things mixed up.

Sophie What things? What are you talking about?

Jen Look, this is ridiculous, I'm probably totally wrong, but I just ...

Pause

She looks like the girl who attacked me last night.

Sophie What — why do you say that?

Jen I just ... she looks the same. Same clothes, same hair ...

Sophie Are you sure?

Jen I don't know. It was dark, but ... Look, it's not, she's your sister, it's ridiculous.

Sophie She told me she's not into that any more.

Jen Into what?

Sophie Look, I haven't seen Alex for four years. There's stuff you don't know about her ... about us.

Jen I don't know anything about her.

Sophie She ... went off the rails. She just turned up here looking for somewhere to stay. She told me she'd changed.

Jen What if she hasn't?

Sophie She promised me.

Jen But what if she hasn't?

Sophie I told her I'd kick her out.

Jen She just said she was in town last night.

Sophie That'd be one hell of a coincidence, to mug my flatmate the night before bumping in to me.

Jen But she tried to lie about being here.

Sophie She just got mixed up.

Jen Mixed up? Either she was here or she wasn't!
Sophie She explained what happened.
Jen How do we find out?
Sophie Find out what?
Jen If it was her.
Sophie I don't know ... ask her?
Jen Oh well done Miss Marple, that'll work — "Excuse me, Alex, but I was just wondering, did you assault me last night?"
Sophie Don't be sarcastic.
Jen I'm sorry Soph, but I was mugged last night, and I don't care whether she's your sister or not, I don't want to spend all evening socializing with my attacker.

Alex enters

Alex Do you want sugar?
Sophie No thanks.

Alex catches Jen's eye, and exits to the kitchen

Jen It's her. It's definitely her.
Sophie You don't know that.
Jen I was there.
Sophie You said it was dark.
Jen I could still see.
Sophie You said it happened quickly.
Jen It did, but ... look, OK, it might be her, it might not be her, but either way I'd like to know.
Sophie Let me talk to her then.
Jen Well I'd quite like to ——
Sophie Let *me* talk to her first, OK?

Beat

Jen And if it's her?
Sophie I don't know. We'll deal with it.

Jen stares at Sophie

Jen You've got five minutes.

Jen gets up and goes to her room

Alex enters with a cup of tea for Sophie

Alex What was that about?
Sophie What?
Alex I'm not stupid. You wanted me out the room for a reason.
Sophie I wanted to apologize for you being rude.
Alex I wasn't rude.
Sophie You were aggressive.
Alex She was staring — you saw it.
Sophie Maybe a bit.
Alex And you apologized?

Beat

What else?
Sophie Nothing.
Alex That was it?
Sophie I wanted to check she was OK with you being here.
Alex You'd already checked.
Sophie I wanted to make sure.
Alex Make sure about something you'd already checked?
Sophie Look, if you're going to be antagonistic all week you might as well go now. I'm doing you a favour when most people would've told you to get lost. I haven't seen you for four years. I don't know what you've been up to, but I'm still prepared to help you. Don't forget that.

Pause

Alex Don't you have a TV?

Sophie I don't watch TV.

Pause

Why are you here?
Alex I've already said.
Sophie Yeah, but why are you *really* here?
Alex I told you.
Sophie You said you needed a place to stay, you haven't said why.
Alex I want to change. (*Pause*) I got mixed up with the wrong people. I wanted to get away from them and you were the only person I could think of to go to.
Sophie Who were these people?
Alex The people I lived with.
Sophie What sort of people were they?
Alex I dunno. I suppose we were sort of a "gang".
Sophie What sort of "gang"?
Alex Nothing serious. We just hung about, like you do.
Sophie Doing what?
Alex Stuff.
Sophie Hanging round on street corners?
Alex Sort of.
Sophie Drinking?
Alex Sometimes.
Sophie Fighting?
Alex Doing what gangs do!
Sophie And you've done this for four years?
Alex I worked for a bit.
Sophie Where?
Alex In an offy. Sophie, I want to change. Can't you see that? I've left all that behind, and I wanna start again.
Sophie Where were you last night?
Alex What?
Sophie Where were you last night? You told me you saw me yesterday, and then you told Jen that you'd just arrived. Nothing adds up.

Alex Yeah, and then I told you I stayed with a friend.
Sophie You said you don't have any friends — I'm the only one you could turn to. If you didn't go back to your own house, and you weren't here, where were you?

Pause

Alex I slept in the park, all right?
Sophie Outside?
Alex There's a shelter there, I slept under that.
Sophie Why didn't you come here? You knew where I was.
Alex I didn't think about it.
Sophie You'd just followed me home.
Alex I didn't want to turn up on your doorstep late at night.
Sophie So you thought you'd prise open my window whilst I was at work instead?
Alex Does it matter?
Sophie Last night Jen got mugged and she thinks it was you who did it.
Alex What?
Sophie She thinks you attacked her.
Alex For fuck's sake, I've only just met the girl and she's accusing me of mugging her! Why's she saying that? Is it, what, 'cos I'm wearing a hood? 'Cos I look slightly out of place next to your elegant furniture?
Sophie She didn't say she was sure, she said her mind might be playing tricks and she just wanted me to ask.
Alex You just accused me ——
Sophie I didn't accuse you, I asked you.
Alex You basically think I've done it.
Sophie No. No one's *accusing* you of anything. As I said, she might be imagining things.
Alex I hope you told her I wouldn't do something like that.

Beat

You did tell her that, didn't you?

Sophie I didn't know what to say.
Alex Thanks.
Sophie You didn't do it then?
Alex Of course I fuckin' didn't.
Sophie Alex!
Alex I didn't do it, all right?! I don't do that.
Sophie I just wanted to make sure.
Alex Well now you know.
Sophie And I believe you.
Alex I don't do that sort of thing.
Sophie OK.
Alex I looked you in the eye earlier and ——
Sophie All right! Relax. I'll tell her it was a mistake.
Alex Tell her it's her turn to apologize.
Sophie I'm sure she will.
Alex Is that why she went off?
Sophie Yes. She's only in her room.

Beat

I'm sorry if that all came out wrong. I didn't mean to sound like I'd cast judgement already.
Alex It's all right. Look, do you wanna go out for a drink or something, just to get out of here?
Sophie I don't drink.
Alex They serve soft drinks in a pub you know.
Sophie I know, it's just not really my scene.
Alex Well, do you want to go somewhere? *Anywhere ...*
Sophie I've got work tomorrow.
Alex No social life, and no TV. This is gonna be fun.

A mobile phone rings in Alex's bag. She picks the phone out of her bag

As she does this, Jen enters holding a portable phone to her ear. She stares at Alex, then stops the call

Jen Why have you got my phone?

Pause

Alex This ain't your phone.
Jen I've just rung my phone and it's gone off in your bag. Why have you got it?
Alex This ain't ... I just found it.
Jen Don't fuck with me / or I'm gonna call the police.
Sophie Jen, calm down.
Alex I just found it, honest to God I just found it.
Jen Oh, big coincidence. Where did you find it? And this better be a fucking good / answer ...
Sophie Jen, *calm down!*
Alex In the park, it was on the ground.
Jen What, you just found a phone in the park lying on the ground / just like that?
Alex I swear.
Jen And what else did you find? Eh? My bag? My money?
Sophie Jen, wait, let's sort this out, there's / no need to ——
Jen Oh I think we've pretty much sorted this out already.
Alex You ain't proved nothing.
Jen I get assaulted last night, get my phone nicked and she turns up at our house a day later with my phone in her bag, I think we've sorted this out.
Alex I found your fucking phone on the floor, how many more times do I have to say it?
Jen Oh right, so the girl who mugged me and stole my phone is just gonna throw the thing on the floor straight after, is she?
Alex Looks that way, love.
Jen WHAT?!
Sophie STOP IT! Calm down. You're in my house and you're behaving like children.
Alex She's accusing me of something I ain't done.

Jen makes a lunge to grab Alex's bag

Jen Give us your bag.

Alex gets there first and snatches it away

Alex Fuck off.
Jen Show us what's in it.
Alex I ain't showing you nothing.
Jen What've you got to hide?
Alex Nothing, I'm just not showing you my bag.
Sophie Jen, just back off, both of you sit down and we'll sort this out.
Jen Get her to empty her bag, and I'll sit down.
Sophie Alex, just empty your bag, if you've got nothing to hide, just empty it and calm this down.
Alex I don't have to do nothing for you, I don't have to / do nothing for her.
Sophie *I think you owe me a lot.*

Silence. Suddenly, Alex throws her bag into the middle of the room

Alex Have it.

Jen picks it up and turns it upside down. Various items including a hammer and a purse fall to the floor. Jen picks up the purse

Jen And that'll be mine as well.
Sophie Alex?

Alex ignores her

Jen (*to Sophie*) Do you want to call the police or shall I?
Sophie No one's calling the police.
Jen You're just gonna let her get away with it?
Sophie I'm not doing anything. I just don't want to get the police involved.
Jen She assaulted me.

Sophie She's my sister.
Jen Some sister! One who disappears for four years and you never talk about.
Sophie She's still family.

Pause

Is anything else missing? Is all your money there?

Jen checks inside her purse

Jen Yeah, I think so.
Sophie Let me try and sort this out. I'm not defending her, I just think ... that at the moment it'd be more productive for *me* to chat to her. You need to calm down a bit.
Jen Don't tell me to calm down.
Sophie You *do*.

Sophie gets closer to Jen and holds her hands

Just ... give us a minute alone. Let me deal with this. Please?

Eventually, Jen turns away and exits

Sophie turns to Alex

You told me you didn't do this any more. You told me you'd given this up. All night you've been standing there saying that you need my help, that you're trying to start again, and all night you've stood there knowing what you did last night. You've done nothing but lie to me since you arrived. And you know the thing is, the thing that makes me angriest of all is that I believed you. (*Pause*) ARE YOU GOING TO SAY ANYTHING? Or are you just going to stand there like a child?
Alex I'm sorry.
Sophie What was that?

Alex I said I'm sorry.

Sophie At last, something human. Although to be quite honest I don't think you mean it.

Alex I mean it.

Sophie Well I hope to God you do, because I've got a good mind to throw you straight back out on the streets. Why did you lie to me?

Alex I didn't mean to.

Sophie Then what did you mean?

Alex I meant what I said. I want to change. I didn't lie to you about that.

Sophie No, you're just lying to yourself.

Alex I know what it looks like. But I'm not. And yeah, I've probably screwed it up, but that doesn't mean I still don't need your help.

Sophie I think you need to tell me everything, because right now none of this makes any sense. You told me you saw me yesterday, but didn't want to knock on my door. Then, somehow, you managed to mug my housemate before deciding it would be a good idea to wrench open my window with a hammer you happen to be carrying and wait for me to come home from work.

Alex That's not the way it happened.

Sophie Then start from the beginning. Jen wants to call the police on you by the way, so remember that.

Alex Please don't let her do that.

Sophie That's up to her.

Beat

I'm listening.

Alex It was chance, OK? It was just chance.

Sophie What do you mean?

Alex That I'm here, that I found you. I've been on the streets for two weeks. The people I was squatting with ... the gang ... were all right to start with, but they made me do stuff, you know, to get them money to buy drugs. They forced me to mug people and steal stuff and I was too scared not to. They'd given me a home, you know, and they were all I knew. But I wanted to get away, even though I had nowhere to go. Anyway, a couple of weeks ago things changed. They wanted me to do other stuff.

Sophie What stuff?

Alex You know ... *stuff*.

Sophie Alex? You didn't, did you?

Alex What d'ya think I am? Of course I didn't. That's why I had to get out. I had nothing, no money, nothing. I tried hostels and stuff but nowhere would take me, so I got out of town.

Sophie And then what happened?

Alex I was on the streets.

Sophie Doing what?

Alex Living.

Sophie In the middle of winter, with nothing?

Alex Some people were kind. They'd stop and give me a couple of quid, or get me a cup of tea, but most ignored me. I survived doing the only thing I knew — I mugged people, took their money and moved on.

Sophie How could you do that?

Alex It was that or starve.

Beat

I had to, Soph. I had to.

Sophie So when did you see me?

Alex What do you mean?

Sophie You said you saw me yesterday. When did you spot me?

Alex I didn't.

Sophie You said you did.

Alex I didn't. I lied. I didn't see you.

Sophie So ... what?

Alex I told you. It was chance. Pure chance. I'd found my way to this town, and found the shelter in the park. And Soph, I was cold, *so* cold, I couldn't feel anything. And I was hungry. I thought I was going to die. Then this girl came past, and she looked at me like I was scum, this nasty look as if she hated everything about me, and I thought "I'm gonna do you". I followed her for a bit, and she didn't hear me as I crept up behind her. She put up a bit of a struggle when I tried to snatch her bag away, so I punched her and put her to the floor. I threatened her with a hammer before taking her stuff and running off. Soph, I never use violence.

Sophie That was Jen, wasn't it?

Alex I know that now.

Sophie I can't believe this.

Alex It's the truth. Everything I'm telling you is the truth.

Sophie So then what happened?

Alex When I'd got away I went through her bag and found her purse. I just needed the money to get something to eat. And I couldn't believe it when I opened it up. Right there, inside, was a picture of you and her. She's got it in her purse, you can check. I couldn't believe it. There, staring back at me, at a time when I needed someone, just anyone, was my sister.

Beat

Sophie The sister you'd scarred for life.

Beat

Alex Yeah.

Silence. Alex drops her head. Sophie stares at her. Eventually ...

All night I'm thinking I've gotta make a choice. Do I keep going on as I am in the hope that one day I'll be all right? Or do I try to find my sister and hope that she'll forgive me? I couldn't go on as I was, Sophie. I wanted to change. I got Jen's address from her driving licence, so I thought I could find her and give her her stuff back. Maybe she'd tell me where I could find you. I waited across the street for her to come out this morning, but the first person I saw was you. You didn't see me. I just froze. It was the first time I'd seen you in the flesh, you know, with ... with the ...

Sophie With the scar.

Alex Yeah. I didn't know whether to follow you, or wait to see Jen. And by then you'd gone. Jen must've left before you though 'cos I waited for another couple of hours before coming in.

Sophie Why did you break in?

Alex I was hungry. And cold. (*Beat*) And that's why I'm here. (*Beat*) I'm sorry I wrecked your window.

Silence

Sophie Why didn't you tell me all this before?

Alex I couldn't.

Sophie Why did you stand there and lie to me?

Alex You said you'd kick me out if I was a criminal. I couldn't just tell you that I'd mugged your flatmate, could I?

Sophie But you knew Jen was coming home.

Alex I didn't think she'd recognize me. I was just going to give her stuff back and pretend I'd found it all somewhere.

Pause

Sophie Why should I believe you?

Alex What do you mean?

Sophie You've lied to me all night. Who's to say this isn't another made up story?

Alex What would be the point in that? There's no point in trying to prove it to you. Believe me if you want to.

Pause

Sophie Did you think I'd forgiven you?

Alex I hoped. Have you?

Sophie I don't know. I've tried to.

Alex And?

Sophie I think to forgive you have to understand. God tells me to forgive you every day, but ... I don't know. I've never felt able to. I think it's because I've never understood why you hurt me.

Beat

What happened to you, Alex?

Jen enters

Jen Has she said anything yet?
Alex I *can* hear you, you know. You *can* talk to me.
Jen Maybe I don't want to. (*To Sophie*) What's the deal?
Sophie We've talked.
Jen And?
Sophie She admits what she did was wrong.
Jen Einstein give her a hand working that one out, did he?
Sophie She came here to give you your stuff back.
Jen What?
Sophie She came here to return your things.
Jen Give me a break. She got found out, it was bad luck.
Sophie It's the truth.
Jen It's what she told you, that doesn't mean anything.
Sophie If that's what you think ——
Jen And what else has she told you?
Alex Hello? I am here you know.
Jen (*to Alex*) Listen, she might be defending you, but I don't care — I don't believe a word you're saying.
Alex You haven't even heard me say anything.
Jen Actions speak louder than words.
Alex Give me a break.
Jen All right. All right, I'll listen to you. I'll listen, but I don't want her in here.
Alex Eh?
Jen I want to talk. You and me.
Sophie You think I'm going to leave you two alone?
Jen She had me to herself last night, and I want her to myself now.
Sophie No way! I've had enough of all this for one night. No more.
Jen I'm not going to get angry. I just want to talk to her. (*To Alex*) I think I'm owed that.

Sophie Why are you doing this?
Alex It's OK. She's right. Leave us.

Pause

Sophie I'll be in my room. If I hear so much as a raised voice ...

Sophie exits

Jen Come on then.
Alex What?
Jen Tell me the truth.
Alex I'm sorry for what I did, OK? But like she said, I came here to give you your stuff back.
Jen Bollocks.
Alex It's the truth.
Jen Bullshit. I didn't exactly notice you present me with my stuff the moment I walked in. No, I had to ring my own phone and empty your / bag myself.
Alex Exactly! Why would I walk into your house with your phone, with your SIM card still in it, and leave it on? Any idiot who's stolen a phone knows not to do that.
Jen Why did you take it in the first place?

Pause

It's not so easy, is it, standing face to face with your victim? Simple to spin Sophie a line and make out you're sorry, but when you have to look into the eye of someone you've hurt it's suddenly not so easy.
Alex Believe me, it ain't easy to look my sister in the eye.

Pause

Jen I'm sick of your type.
Alex What's my type?
Jen You know.

Alex No, I don't.

Jen The "youth" of today. You walk around town with your baseball caps on and your hoods up and you think you can get away with anything. But you're weak.

Alex You don't know anything about me.

Jen I know you mug people and threaten them with hammers. That's enough for me.

Alex Then maybe you're the weak one.

Jen No. People don't do things like that unless it's in their nature, unless it's part of them, inside them.

Alex And maybe it's people like you who put it there.

Jen Yeah that's right. That's the easy way out — blame someone else. Can't you take responsibility for your own actions? Do you always have to find someone else to blame? That's what's happening, you see? That's the world in which we live — nothing's ever our fault anymore. You run out in front of a car, and it's the driver's fault for not seeing you. You fail your exams and it's your teacher's fault for not doing their job. You batter your wife but it was justified because she realized you were a nasty piece of work and ended up shagging the milkman. And do you know what? Most people get away with it. Sometimes they get a fat cheque to compensate for their own inadequacy. And that makes me sick.

Alex I'm not blaming anyone else.

Jen Yes you are! You just said it's people like me that make others act the way they do.

Alex Sometimes people aren't free to act the way they want to.

Jen What's that supposed to mean?

Alex Sometimes we do things we know are wrong, but it's the only choice we have.

Jen There's always an alternative.

Alex In your life, maybe.

Beat

Jen So what made you do what you did last night?

Alex I needed money. I'm on the streets.

Jen You could've asked politely.

Alex Yeah right, 'cos that would've worked. I saw you looking at me. I saw what you were thinking, exactly what you've just said, that I was trash, scum of the / earth, dirty ——

Jen You're doing it again. You're blaming me. So what? I looked at you. That doesn't mean you have to threaten me with a hammer.

Alex No, but it makes it a good option.

Jen Why can't you just be honest and say, "I'm a bad person".

Alex Because I'm not.

Jen Go on, say it. "I'm a bad person".

Alex No.

Jen Go on.

Alex I'm not.

Jen Go on! "I'm a bad person".

Alex Shut up.

Jen "I live on the streets and blame others and I'm a bad person".

Alex SHUT UP!

Jen "I threaten innocent people with hammers and fuck their lives up / and I'm a bad person".

Alex IF YOU DON'T SHUT UP ——

Jen Admit it to yourself. Say it with me — I'm — a — bad ——

Alex SHUT THE FUCK UP OR I'LL DO TO YOU WHAT I DID TO SOPHIE.

Sophie bursts in

Jen And that was ...?

Jen looks at Sophie. She suddenly realizes

(*To Alex*) And you think there's nothing wrong with you?

Alex starts to break down

Sophie I knew it was a bad idea to leave you two alone.

Sophie goes to Alex and holds her

Alex (*crying*) I'm sorry.
Sophie Come on, sit down.
Alex I'm sorry for what I did.
Sophie It's all right.
Alex It ain't all right. Look what I've done to you.
Sophie Shh.
Alex I've hurt you.
Sophie It's OK.
Alex Every day for the last four years I've wanted to see you again but I've been scared to find you 'cos I'd have to look at what I'd done.
Jen Why did she do that to you?
Alex Soph, I've gone through hell these last few years, and the only thing that's kept me going is the thought that it's nowhere near the hell you must've been through.
Sophie Why did you do it?
Alex I can't tell you.
Sophie I want to know.
Alex If I told you it'd make it worse.
Sophie Alex, I have to know.
Alex Look at you. And look at me. And we're sisters. We have nothing in common. You're so successful, so ... normal. And I'm a wreck.
Sophie Don't say that.
Alex It's true.
Sophie But it wasn't like that when we were at home.
Alex Were you blind?! How can you say that? You were the popular one. Mum always favoured you, she gave you everything. You did well at school, had great friends, everyone loved you, and I was this spotty little rat with greasy hair who got picked on all the time.
Sophie You had friends.
Alex I was a laughing stock.
Sophie And so you took a knife to my face?
Alex Five years at school living in your shadow, five years of getting beaten up 'cos I was ugly.
Sophie You didn't get beaten up.
Alex You were never there for me.
Sophie Don't say that.

Alex It's true. I hated my life and I blamed you for it.
Sophie Why didn't you talk to me?
Alex I couldn't. You were so wrapped up in other stuff, in God, that you had no idea what was going on around you.
Sophie You still could've talked to me.
Alex And one day I just flipped. I can't tell you why 'cos I don't know myself. But I just knew I had to get away. I don't know what made me do what I did. It felt like revenge for all the beatings I'd had because I wasn't as beautiful as you.

Beat

Sophie Is that all it was?
Alex Yes.
Sophie You disfigured me because of how I looked.
Alex No, because of how I looked.
Jen Here we go again.
Alex You asked me why I did it. I'm only telling you what I thought.

Beat

Jen (*to Sophie*) Are you going to sit there and take that?
Sophie What do you mean?
Jen Are you going to sit there and let her feed you this rubbish?
Alex What's it got to do with you?
Jen (*to Sophie*) She sliced your face with a knife.
Sophie I know what she did. I'm well aware of what she did. But what can I do about it? For a year afterwards all I heard people say to me was "Are you OK?" Are you OK?! Of course I'm not OK. But it's happened. It's done. I can't change it.
Jen I don't know how you can sit there with her.
Alex What's it got to do with you?
Jen I think you're forgetting the small matter that I was mugged by you last night.
Alex I think we're dealing with slightly more important things than you right now.

Jen You still don't seem to grasp what you've done.
Alex I know what I've done.
Jen That's easy for you to say, but what scars do you have to bear?
Alex Plenty.
Jen So you say.
Alex So what do you want then? Eh? What do you want?

Suddenly, Alex grabs the hammer that was lying on the floor. She gives it to Jen and kneels in front of her

Go on then! If that's what you want. Revenge. You've been wanting to do this all night, what are you waiting for? Go on. DO IT!

Jen suddenly makes a move as if to hit her, but doesn't

Sophie NO!

Pause

Jen drops the hammer to the floor. She picks up the phone and dials

Jen (*into the phone*) Police.

Alex looks at Sophie

Sophie Jen, no!

Sophie goes to Jen and tries to wrestle the phone away from her. Alex pulls Sophie away

Alex Let her.
Sophie They'll take you away.
Jen (*into the phone*) I'd like to report a theft and an assault. The assailant is in my house. (*Beat*) It's OK, she's not going anywhere. I just need help. (*Beat*) R-G-nineteen, five-R-T. Twenty-five. (*Beat*) Thank you.

The following dialogue happens over Jen's phone call

Sophie I'll stand up for you.
Alex There's no point in lying.
Sophie They can't take you away.

Pause

Alex Soph, do you believe what I've told you?
Sophie Yes.
Alex You know, I think God wanted me to find you. I think He showed me your picture. He wanted to show me that out of something bad something good can happen. I called it chance, but maybe it was a miracle. I'm sorry for all this.

They hug

I need to use the toilet.

Alex exits to the bathroom

Jen hangs up the phone. Long pause

Jen I had to do it. For both of us.
Sophie For you. I've made my peace.
Jen Good for you.
Sophie I think somewhere in all this you've lost sight of the fact that she's my sister.
Jen And I mean nothing to you?
Sophie For all her faults, she's family.

Long pause. Eventually, Sophie heads towards the bathroom

Jen Where are you going?
Sophie To check she's OK.
Jen Great. I'm fine by the way.
Sophie You got what you wanted.

Sophie exits

Jen (*calling after her*) Sophie ...

Pause. After a short while, the sound of a door being forced from off

Eventually, Sophie hurries back

Sophie She's gone.
Jen What?
Sophie She's gone!
Jen What do you mean she's gone?
Sophie The window's wide open and she's not in there.
Jen Well where's she gone?
Sophie I don't know, she's run off.

She puts on her coat and grabs her keys off the table

Jen What are you doing?
Sophie I'm going after her.

Jen stops her

Jen There's no point.
Sophie She can't have gone far.
Jen It's pointless. She's running away, she doesn't want to be found.
Sophie I need to find her.
Jen If she wanted you to follow her she wouldn't have climbed out the window.
Sophie She's got nothing, she needs me.
Jen Sophie, listen ––
Sophie It was a miracle she said, and she found me. I was supposed to help her and we've turned her away.
Jen She ran away.
Sophie Because of us.
Jen Don't blame me for this.
Sophie I'm blaming both of us.

Jen What did I do?!

Sophie I thought we were friends.

Jen You're not answering me.

Sophie I thought I could rely on you, I thought I could trust you and you stab me in the back. Get off me!

Jen You've lost the plot.

Sophie You did this.

Jen What?!

Sophie You made her run away. You scared her.

Jen How?

Sophie I've forgiven her. Do you know that? I've forgiven her for what she did to me, but thanks to you I'll never be able to tell her.

Jen WHAT DID *I* DO?!

Sophie You called the police on her. How could you do that?! You called the police on her, you ——

Jen I didn't call the police.

Beat

Sophie What?

Jen I didn't call the police. I pretended to.

Sophie I heard you, I saw you do it.

Jen Are you listening to me? I didn't dial a number. I pretended. OK? I didn't call them. I was gonna tell you.

Sophie Why did you do that?

Jen Why do you think? At some point, Sophie, she's gonna have to stand up and take responsibility for what she's done. She can't blame others. I wouldn't have called the police on her, she's your sister. But I wanted her to know I could've.

Pause

Sophie Get out.

Jen What?

Sophie Get *out!* Pack your stuff and get out.

Jen Why?

Sophie I don't want you in my house.

Jen That's right, make me the scapegoat.
Sophie GET OUT!
Jen And then what? Then she might come back? Get real! She wanted to use you Sophie, nothing more. Don't delude yourself.
Sophie You've made your point, but my sister's gone because of you.
Jen And she'll come running back as soon as she's in trouble again. She knows where to find you. You can't chase her.
Sophie I'll do what I like.
Jen You're wasting your time.

Beat

Sophie I think you should leave.
Jen Why are you doing this?
Sophie I can't look at you.
Jen So that's what this comes to? You're insane. That's how little I mean to you ——
Sophie Please, GO!
Jen Don't worry, I'm going. Thanks for your support.

Jen turns to leave, then pauses

You know, it's funny how, despite seeming so totally opposite, you and her are actually pretty much the same. Blaming others. (*Looking up*) He hasn't actually taught you very much, has He?

Jen exits to her bedroom

Sophie is left alone, deflated. She thinks, then takes off her coat and puts down her keys. As she does so, she sees her bible. She picks it up from the coffee table and looks at it, as if to find some inspiration

Black-out

CURTAIN

FURNITURE AND PROPERTY LIST

On stage: Coat stand
Sofa
Coffee table. *On it*: bible, picture of **Sophie** and her mum
Side table. *On it*: telephone
Bag (for **Alex**), containing mobile phone, hammer, purse and various other items

Offstage: Pyjamas, toothbrush (**Sophie**)
Cheese (**Jen**)
Portable phone (**Jen**)
Cup of tea (**Alex**)

Personal: **Sophie**: keys
Alex: cigarette, lighter

LIGHTING PLOT

Practical fittings required: nil

To open: Darkness, with light from a street lamp spilling in from outside

Cue 1	**Sophie** switches on the light *Bring up Lights*	(Page 1)
Cue 2	**Sophie** picks up the bible and looks at it *Black-out*	(Page 37)

EFFECTS PLOT

Cue 1 To open, after a long pause (Page 1)
We hear a front door open and shut

Cue 2 **Alex**: "Jen what?" (Page 9)
A door opens and closes off stage

Cue 3 **Jen**: "I'm gonna get some food." (Page 10)
A toilet flushes off stage

Cue 4 **Alex**: "This is gonna be fun." (Page 19)
A mobile phone rings in **Alex***'s bag*

Cue 5 **Jen**: "Sophie ..." (Page 35)
A pause, then the sound of a door being forced from off

Printed by The Kingfisher Press, London NW10 7AS